BY MALLORY ERVIN

Living Fully

All In

All In

All In

A VISION FOR LIVING FULLY EVERY DAY

Mallory Ervin

CONVERGENT

New York

Published in the United States by Convergent Books, an imprint of
Random House, a division of Penguin Random House LLC, New York.

CONVERGENT BOOKS is a registered trademark and its C colophon is a
trademark of Penguin Random House LLC.

LIBRARY OF CONGRESS CATALOGING-IN-PUBLICATION DATA
Names: Ervin, Mallory, author.
Title: All in / Mallory Ervin.
Description: New York : Convergent, [2023]
Identifiers: LCCN 2022036806 (print) | LCCN 2022036807 (ebook) |
ISBN 9780593238363 (hardcover) | ISBN 9780593238370 (ebook)
Subjects: LCSH: Self-actualization (Psychology) | Joy. | Self-realization.
Classification: LCC BF637.S4 E767 2023 (print) | LCC BF637.S4 (ebook) |
DDC 158.1–dc23/eng/20220829
LC record available at https://lccn.loc.gov/2022036806
LC ebook record available at https://lccn.loc.gov/2022036807

Printed in the United States of America on acid-free paper

crownpublishing.com

1st Printing

First Edition

Book design by Debbie Glasserman

To my daughter,
Sunday.

You're
my dream
come true.

Contents

I discovered that we can't find a full life in those "hero moments" just as we can't find it in the "zero moments." Instead, we find it in a practice, a constant way of life. That practice is living fully. And it leads not to a specific destination, goal, or achievement, but instead, back to the best version of yourself.

Introduction

Maybe you found your way to this book after reading my first one, **_Living Fully._** Maybe you never heard of me before and someone just slapped this book in your lap and told you to read it. Regardless of how you came to discover these pages, one thing is the same for all of us: We all have a desire to live a life that we feel is a full one. We all want a happy life. A fulfilling life. A successful life. And depending on who you ask, the definition of a full life looks very different for each of us. However, I think most of us spend most of our time thinking about those hero moments as we work to live fully. Those times when we're really crushing it at work, when we're being exactly the kind of parent we want to be and taking our children on adventures that are meaningful and worthy of a place on our Instagram grid, or finally achieving a big goal like completing a marathon.

The thing is, living fully isn't temporary, just something to pull us out of those moments when we feel we've hit rock bottom. And it isn't something we embrace when we feel like we're on top of the world. So, if you're reading this book to try to figure out how to get rich quick, find the love of your life, get the body of your dreams by your high school reunion, or something else like that, this isn't for you. Living fully is about finding those things that make you feel fulfilled, and finding your groove in the way it feels best for you to live. Those are things that only you can articulate, and a one-size-fits-all approach to living fully simply doesn't work. Striving to live a full life means that you're not just working toward the next reaching-the-mountaintop experience, but you're working to make every day meaningful, fulfilling, and life-giving. Living fully means living fully **every day,** and finding that joy and purpose in your everyday life.

66

My goal is to guide you to purposely seek out the answers you're looking for. Now that I have found my purpose, I get out of bed every day with both feet on the ground, ready to live my best life. It is messy, joyous, and, yes, chaotic at times. But I love it and wouldn't have it any other way. I am living fully, and I can't wait to help you do the same.

Now I'm no longer in pursuit of big things but a big life. And in that big life, what's important is the everyday.

99

I'll be honest. From the outside, the "everyday" can seem like the opposite of the razzle-dazzle, but it is far from it. The times in the middle of our big highs and lows are actually the exciting parts! Living fully doesn't necessarily mean you spend every day traveling to some exotic location, constantly having a perfectly curated social media grid, or having a house that's always spotless and perfectly on-trend. If you read *Living Fully,* you know that I spent a lot of time journeying through addiction, self-doubt, and a ton of lows to finally build a life for myself where I feel like every day is life-giving and fulfilling. Does that mean my life is perfect? Far from it! Does it mean every day is a good one and I'm always happy? Whew! I wish that were true. But what it does mean is that I've figured out what I need to be the best version of myself and how to choose my own happy. It helps me use my energy on things that build me and my family up rather than spending my energy trying to meet someone else's view of perfection, happiness, or success.

The process was so life-changing for me, and has made my life fuller and more beautiful than I could have ever imagined. I wrote my first book because living fully made such an impact on my life, and I wanted others to experience that too. My desire behind this book is no different, I want **you** to be able to live fully, but I know you may be thinking, "Good Lord, where do I even start?" That's where this book comes in. I know you have the desire and the drive to live a beautiful, full life, and all you need is someone to just point you in the right direction and empower you to start making bold choices. I'm not going to just give you suggestions on how to visualize ways you can start living fully; I'm also going to help you visualize what you want your life to look like, and ways you can spend every day working toward those goals.

I don't want this book to just be another thing that sits, unused, on your shelf. Instead, I want you to find hope, inspiration, and empowerment to finally find a way to build the life you were meant to live and make lasting, meaningful changes. I hope as we walk through these pages together I can help you not only by just giving you a wake-up call to change your life but also by helping you stay awake to continue along this path as you're living it. I want this book to be your stay-awake call, and I want these pages to offer you tangible, accessible ways to live fully every day.

Before we get going, I want you to take a moment to take stock of where you are right now.

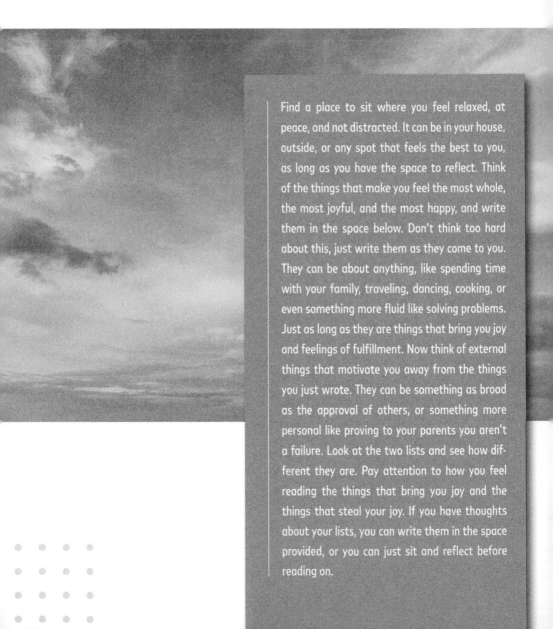

Find a place to sit where you feel relaxed, at peace, and not distracted. It can be in your house, outside, or any spot that feels the best to you, as long as you have the space to reflect. Think of the things that make you feel the most whole, the most joyful, and the most happy, and write them in the space below. Don't think too hard about this, just write them as they come to you. They can be about anything, like spending time with your family, traveling, dancing, cooking, or even something more fluid like solving problems. Just as long as they are things that bring you joy and feelings of fulfillment. Now think of external things that motivate you away from the things you just wrote. They can be something as broad as the approval of others, or something more personal like proving to your parents you aren't a failure. Look at the two lists and see how different they are. Pay attention to how you feel reading the things that bring you joy and the things that steal your joy. If you have thoughts about your lists, you can write them in the space provided, or you can just sit and reflect before reading on.

Reflect

All In

"

Shake off that impostor syndrome, shush that negative voice in your head telling you this nonsense, and tell yourself that your dreams, goals, and desires are valid and worth fighting for.

"

01

MORE THAN WISHFUL THINKING

hances are, you've heard someone casually talking about visualizing, or manifesting, something into their lives. It's one of those concepts people like to throw around a lot, and depending on who you're talking to, it can mean a variety of different things. I also know that people can write off visualization as a woo-woo practice that doesn't really have much bearing on your life. I suppose some people consider manifesting something they don't really understand or have access to. But for me? Manifesting has been literally life-changing, and deeply rooted in my life since I was a child. And it's something that I want to help you bring into your own life. You deserve to live fully, and you deserve to have good things in your life, even if they might feel like big, audacious goals. I want you to feel empowered here and excited about naming those things you want in your life. I want to help you make tangible plans every day to manifest them. I'm going to help you create a tool to do just that, and I know it's going to change your life like it's changed mine.

Now don't worry, we aren't talking about magic here. Absolutely not. When I talk about manifesting, about visualization,

> **I'm talking about clearly articulating what it is you want and placing that visual representation of it in a space (or on a vision board) where you see it often and bring it outward from your subconscious.**

If you don't write visualization off as hocus-pocus, it can help you bring a pretty spectacular life to fruition. Visualization is a powerful practice that has recently become more rooted in the science of neuroplasticity–which is the ability the brain has to change. Dr. Tara Swart is a friend of mine who has also been a pioneer in applying visualization to what science understands of neuroplasticity. In the pages that follow, I'll be using some of my tried-and-true techniques that have worked for me to help guide you along your journey to propel you into living fully.

I invite you to leave your skepticism at the door and try to be open to this. **As with anything, your mind-set plays a huge part in how successful a new practice will be in your life.** If you're going to start visualizing the life you want and begin manifesting these things into your life, you can't just simply say, "I want a new car." Like I said, this isn't magic, and visualization isn't as easy as making a wish. You've got to be confident enough to truly envision yourself receiving those things you're trying to manifest in your life.

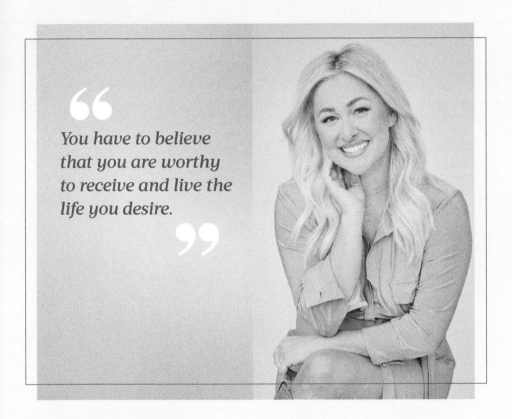

> *You have to believe that you are worthy to receive and live the life you desire.*

You have to believe **to your core** that you are worthy of the achievements and experiences you so desperately want in your life.

If you go into this as a skeptic trying to disprove everything, or if you approach visualizing with a lack of confidence, your success is going to be impacted. However, if you open your mind and your heart, decide to trust the process, and have the confidence that you can achieve the things you are visualizing for your life, you're going to experience a lot more success as you walk this journey. In the pages that follow, you'll set clear intentions and goals for your life, and you'll create your own vision board to help you begin living fully every day. But this is all going to be a pointless exercise for you if you're not **all in**. So, if you're ready to take a step of faith with me, let's get started.

> *Shake off that impostor syndrome, shush that negative voice in your head telling you this nonsense, and tell yourself that your dreams, goals, and desires are valid and worth fighting for.*

Like with any journey, you can't set out successfully if you don't know where you're going, and it's exactly the same with visualization. Visualization begins with deciding what you want in your life. This is the piece a lot of people don't take the time to do. But it's not an option—you have to do this step and do it well. Now, I know if we were sitting at a table together talking through this, your first instinct might be to give me a broad answer. *I want to be happy. I want to own my own business. I want to have a stronger family. I want to be healthier.* Don't get me wrong, these are all great things to want, but you have to get a little more specific so you can actually have a VISION for living fully. These goals and desires are so broad, that getting to the point of happier, healthier, or business owner could look wildly different from day to day. So, when we're working to visualize and manifest things into our lives, we've got to get specific.

Go back to page xvii and look at what you wrote down. I want you to use those answers to begin to really reflect upon what you want out of your life. Before you catch the vision, you have to cast the vision. It's okay to start broad at first, but don't stop there. Get even more specific and start to form sharper images of what you want. To help you do this, I want you to go ahead and focus on what you feel like you truly need in your life and start thinking about some clear goals you can set for yourself. This will get your mind in the right place.

> **Take some time to really think about how you want to feel about yourself and your life. What things make you feel alive and fill your heart with joy? Now think about goals you can set for yourself to help you feel like that every day.**

We're starting on a big project here, and it's important to have all the tools we need before we begin! Living fully is something you'll be working toward every day, so you're not always going to feel like you're unstoppable, on top of the world, or even doing a good job. Being able to look at something that represents how you want your life to make you feel and remind yourself of why you're doing this will help keep you moving forward.

It is also vital to feel good when you're trying to bring good things into your life. And truly understanding the power visualization can hold is not only helpful when you're working to attain goals, but it's also a powerful tool when you find yourself sliding into a place of doubt or spiraling thoughts. We don't want to camp out there. So use visualization to get back on track.

Sometimes I'll picture repetitive negative (or doubting) thoughts like leaves falling from the sky or floating on a river, or I'll envision a big stop sign to **stop** my negative spiral and regain control. You could also create a motto that you can repeat in those moments to help you stop the spiral and get back to where you want to be. Life isn't always going to be easy, and things aren't always going to go as you expect, but if you have reminders that can ground you to your truth, your core values, and what you want out of your life, it can help you stay in control–*before* your life spins into something you no longer recognize.

What are some things you can visualize to help you stay in a positive frame of mind, even when things get chaotic?

Craft a quick life motto, a sort of mantra even, that you can repeat in those moments when you're feeling stuck that can get you back on track.

I want you to circle back to creating the specific goals for yourself, then take it a step further by thinking of what a visual representation of each thing would be. I like to find a visual representation in a picture–rather than words or lists–to put on my vision board. For you it might be a picture from a magazine or a photograph or some type of word art.

Get as precise as possible and try to picture each thing you want as **fully realized in your life**. This is extremely important because it's a big part of what makes your vision board such a powerful tool. Think of it as a **road map,** and a road map isn't helpful if there isn't a clear destination. Think about it: If you had a dream of seeing the Hollywood sign, directions from your house to Los Angeles would get you close, but not to your actual goal. It's the same idea with your vision board.

Once you articulate what you want in your life, you need to find a visual representation of that thing in its fruition.

Here's another thing I'll put on your radar: For years I filled my vision board with pictures that articulated my goals and dreams before they had been fully realized. For example, for over a year, as I worked to grow my family, I would put an ultrasound picture on my vision board to symbolize getting pregnant. And y'all, I did get pregnant. A lot, actually. Four times, to be exact! However, I miscarried each of those four pregnancies. Now, I'm not saying that I did my vision board wrong and caused myself to lose these pregnancies or that there's a medical link to this method. I am saying that there is power in imagining the thing you're trying to manifest, but *more* power in visualizing that thing in fruition. That's where Dr. Tara Swart's studies came into play for me. She helped me understand that because visualization is working hand in hand with my brain, I need to be really clear about how I articulate the things I want to manifest in my life. Since I desired another baby, I changed my vision board, and instead of attaching an ultrasound image, I'd put a picture of my family with another child. If you're visualizing a new house, don't just visualize the house, but visualize your life in that place, and what it is you want that house to bring. Picture your family in the yard, making holiday meals in the kitchen, watching movies with your family in the living room.

I like to think of creating a vision board as almost a prayer in fast-forward, because there is something so powerful about spending time visualizing our desires coming to fruition in our lives. It can make our desires feel so much more real, and it can make us feel so much more grateful for our lives now and for what is to come. It can really let our desires take root in our hearts and give us the confidence to know that this thing will actually come to pass in our lives.

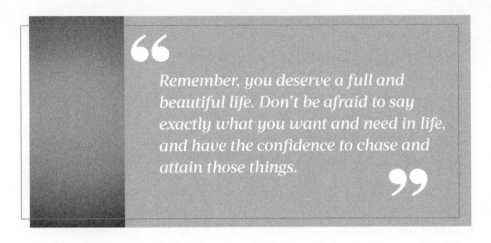

> Remember, you deserve a full and beautiful life. Don't be afraid to say exactly what you want and need in life, and have the confidence to chase and attain those things.

To be clear, visualization doesn't mean that we're magically conjuring something up in our lives. We'll still have to work for it, and we'll still have to live fully and intentionally each day with our core values in mind. But that's why we're taking the time to get our frame of mind in the right place. Visualizing and manifesting the things we desire in our lives are ways of articulating our desires. Really working to visualize these things coming to full fruition in our lives helps us create that road map in our mind as we work each day to attain what we want.

Of course, it can be really tough to follow through with visualization and to keep those goals in the front of your mind every day. That's where a vision board comes in. I've found a vision board to be such a powerful tool because it gives me a place to put those dreams and goals in my life where I can easily see them, remind myself of what I'm working toward, and keep me living fully every day. It's why I want you to develop your own vision board. You'll create this board in whatever way makes sense for you, using whatever supplies you're drawn to. Whether you make it on your computer or you go old-school and create a collage with a poster board, just do something that is meaningful to you. When you're done you'll put it in a place in your home or office that you'll see frequently and be reminded of your goals.

Now don't worry too much. I know we're only at the beginning of this book, so I'm not tossing you into the deep end to create a vision board all at once. You'll start by visioning and making lists, then you'll collect images to transfer to your vision board, and finally you'll assemble your board. For now, start thinking about the best way to take those things from your head and your heart and put them onto a board. For me, especially when I don't know where to start, I've found it easiest to divide my vision board into sections. I've used headers like **house, family,** and **business,** but you'll create whatever sections align with your life. I don't want you to start putting things on your board just yet; we'll get into the how-to of your board in chapter 5, but for now, just let this ruminate.

Continue reflecting on those things that you want to bring into your life. But remember, think about them as if they've come to fruition. If you're like me and you wanted a baby, think about a new child in your family, and what your daily life would look like with a new little one running around. If it's a house or a new place to live, think about where it is you want to live, if you have a specific house in mind, think about being all moved in and experiencing life in that place. If it's a spouse, think about what you want in a partner, and what your life would look life together.

Getting Specific

Look back at your notes on page xvii and those things that you want to bring into your life. But remember, think about them as if they've come to fruition. If you're looking for a spouse, think of finding yourself a teammate, not an unrealistic romance novel ideal of a spouse. For me, I needed someone who truly felt like a partner walking through life with me, and boy, did I find that in Kyle! Because I wasn't just looking for some other pie-in-the-sky guy you find in your favorite rom-com, I was able to find a man who supports me, believes in my goals, makes me laugh, shares my values, and pushes me to be better every day. So, don't be afraid to get specific when you're thinking about what you really need in a spouse.

If you want a new job, think of something that allows you to use your skills in a way that makes you feel proud and fulfilled, that lets you live the life you want, not something that just looks good on paper. What are your skills and passions, and what type of work feels fulfilling to you? What are your family's specific financial needs, and what kind of job is out there that can help you meet those basic needs but also use your talents in a way that gives you life? So much of living fully is regular, day-to-day living, so we can't forget about finding happiness in our everyday lives as we work to live fully.

> I encourage you to really take your time with this process, so, as we walk through these pages together, really dig deep into your desires and dreams and create a vision board that doesn't just look ideal, but also propels you to the life you want. I know it can be tempting to try to zip through all this prep work, so I'm going to challenge you to really take the time to reflect on the things you can visualize while confidently expecting to achieve the things you put on your vision board.

If you're like me, you'll have the overwhelming impulse to fill up every space on your board with an image. However, I'd encourage you to avoid that urge. No one wants a life that is full to the brim with stuff, with no blank spaces, no margins, and no room for the unexpected or the unplanned. If we're visualizing a life jam-packed with stuff, with no space, no room to breathe, and no room to grow, that's what we're going to create. So instead, allow yourself to leave some open spots on your board. I always struggle to avoid seeing that as wasted space, but remember: It is just as important to allow yourself the time to rest and recharge as it is to visualize big things and live fully.

That's because living fully is 95 percent regular, daily life. Every day isn't going to be some out-of-this-world outrageous experience. Part of allowing ourselves to find the joy, beauty, and happiness in the everyday is by allowing ourselves the space to fully experience it. So, **don't be afraid of a little blank space on your vision board because chances are, you'll be thankful for a bit of blank space in your life too.** You never know what that open space might bring into your life.

More than anything, I want you to remember that this board is a road map that we are using to achieve dreams and goals, yes, but it's also going to guide how we live in the everyday. Knowing where we want to go is important, but it's also important to have a philosophy and a set of core values that can get us from one big mountaintop moment of achievement to the next. And those core values can also help us identify the goals and dreams that best align with the life we want to live and the person we want to become. We will get to those in the next chapters, but for now, take a bit more time to think about the things you want in your life, and try to articulate those ideas in as clear a picture as you can.

Begin thinking about specific things you want to manifest in your life. List them here and try to articulate them in as clear a picture as you can. What are some visual representations of those things? Remember you can come back to this list and add to or subtract from it as needed.

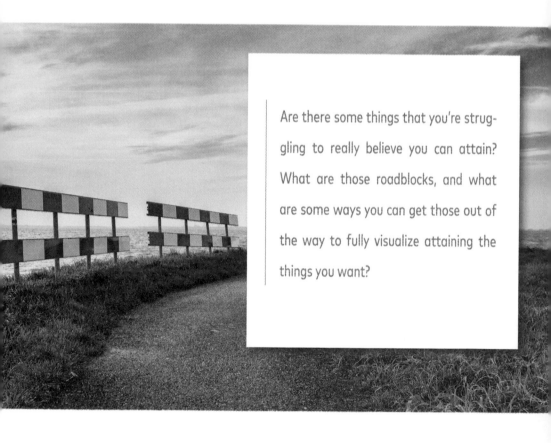

Are there some things that you're struggling to really believe you can attain? What are those roadblocks, and what are some ways you can get those out of the way to fully visualize attaining the things you want?

Reflect

_____
_____
_____
_____
_____
_____
_____
_____
_____
_____
_____
_____
_____
_____

"

The way we choose
to live our days on this
earth can be an inspiration
to others in the present,
not just after we're gone.
By exchanging the belief
that a legacy is something
we leave behind for the
truth that we are living it
right here and now,
we step into our
ability to live fully.

"

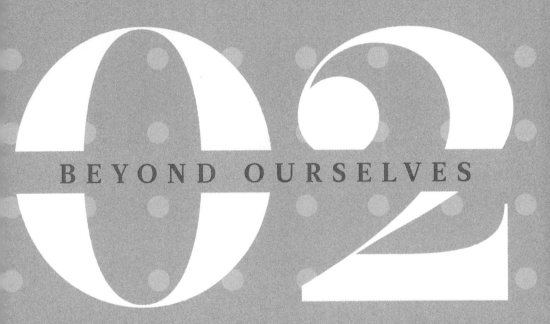

02
BEYOND OURSELVES

I f you've spent any amount of time in the self-help space, chances are you've heard the word **legacy** tossed around quite a bit. It's one of those words that maybe has even started to lose some of its meaning. But living with your legacy in mind is a really important part of living fully. So, what do I mean when I say *legacy?*

Well, just like your life vision, the legacy you want to leave behind is going to be different for every person. But in essence, your legacy is more than just what you want to be remembered for. It's the impact you want to make on the world both now and long after you've passed on. Your legacy should be something you spend every day working toward.

> *As you begin chasing your dreams and creating a vision for the life you want, it is important to make sure the things on your vision board don't just align with your core values and your legacy, but that they help build it.*

Our legacy isn't something we just achieve one day, check a box, and then stop worrying about. If you want to be remembered as a prolific chef, you don't just craft one gourmet meal and call it good. You spend your life honing your craft, studying, and inventing and tweaking recipes, so that when you're gone people will remember you for your amazing culinary skills. But more importantly, you start building that legacy and forging it each day through the fires of experience, trial and error, and through creativity and awareness. A **lasting legacy** is one that you start building during your lifetime and that carries on after you're gone. I like to think of legacy not simply as something that sticks around after I'm gone. I try to think of a **living legacy.** Something I work toward building by the way I show up living my life every single day.

"

The way we choose
to live our days on
this earth can be an
inspiration to others
in the present, not
just after we're gone.
By exchanging the
belief that a legacy is
something we leave
behind for the truth
that we are living it
right here and now,
we step into our
ability to live fully.

"

When we think about living fully, we take the time to assess where we are right now, but we also have to pay attention to the future. We have to visualize where we want our future to head and how our actions are getting us there (or stopping us from reaching our goals), and then pay attention to how our actions right now are building that legacy. How will people describe you today or in five years? How will your spouse describe you to friends and colleagues? How will your children describe you to their friends as they grow? How will family members? How do you want them to see you? The peacekeeper? The safe place? The defender? The nurturer? The problem-solver? Visualize how you want to weave those descriptions into your life more, and ways that you want to see that living legacy play out in your life and the lives of your loved ones.

If you're going to live your life in "legacy mode," working daily to build a living and lasting legacy, you've got to take steps each day to keep walking that path. Living fully and your legacy are unique to you, so an important first step in mapping out your version of legacy mode is to define what your **core values** are. By core values, I mean the things that you value the most at your core, where you center your moral compass, and the foundational things you use to gauge whether your life is moving in the right direction. There isn't a right or wrong answer here. Maybe your core values center around faith, maybe they're around family, maybe they're about living a creative life, securing financial security for your loved ones, having deep friendships, or maybe they're about living a life focused on big-impact projects. Whatever your core values are, take

some time at the end of this chapter to identify and clearly articulate them so you can always keep them in your mind as you move
through each day.

But we just can't stop at identifying our core values. We've got to
look around our life right now and see how our actions, decisions,
and the things we dedicate our time to add to or detract from those
values and our desired legacy. Maybe it's even worth taking the
time to think about how those who love you the most see you. For
me, I know doing this really shifted my view of legacy from that of
achievements and the standards I held myself to.

"

I know that the people around me never saw my ability to do a million things as a badge of honor like I did. I was wearing myself out for nothing. I wasn't tuned in to my true desires or what a full life actually looked like for me, and instead, I was responding to what I thought was expected of me.

"

Our legacy is also forged by the ways we spend our time, and if we're more focused on doing everything we can, collecting as many shiny objects as we can, and being everything to everyone, we can never craft a legacy or a life based on who we truly are and who we are truly meant to be. So, we need to be sure we're not just identifying our core values, but also looking at how those values align with the way we spend our days and what we say yes to.

OBSTACLES TO BUILDING A LIVING LEGACY

The value of saying no and knowing when to say no—that's a topic that gets a lot of airtime. But it also misses the mark a bit. We have to look at what's motivating us to say yes to the point of running ourselves into the ground. Why don't we carefully weigh and prioritize our yeses instead of handing them out to everyone like candy on Halloween? That's the question we need to be asking ourselves.

I don't want you to think that living fully means filling our days with tasks. Sometimes our days get filled up because we aren't being purposeful about how we manage our time and we aren't protecting certain hours for what matters most.

What are the parts of your day that most align with your core values? What makes them align with your values and helps foster your living legacy?

What are the parts of your day that don't align with your core values, and why don't they? How can you remove them from your day, or rework them to better align with your core values?

When we can align our values to our everyday activities, it can set us forward in a whole new direction of unlocking our **living legacy** and **living fully** each day. It has us filling our days with those life-giving things, not using smaller, life-draining tasks to distract us from what we're meant to be doing. **Because when we align our values to the things we do each day, it means that every task and every interaction is not only helping us live fully, but is also actively building that legacy we want to last long after we're gone.**

So we have to look at the choices we make—how we spend our time, even the places we spend our money—and ask ourselves if they are reflecting what is most important to us. The hours we spend in a day are a really clear indicator of what we think is important and worthwhile. Are we wasting most of our precious time here on this earth doing something we don't think is important, or worse, something that totally misaligns with our core values? Then we're not just wasting time, we're building a legacy we don't want and we don't believe in. Instead, we have to decide what our core values are, and then work to make sure our everyday activities are aligning with those values so we live every day in legacy mode.

Reflect

In the space below, write what you believe your core values are, and then rank them from most to least important.

_____

_____

_____

_____

_____

_____

_____

_____

_____

_____

_____

_____

_____

_____

_____

_____

Now think about how those can translate into headers, sections, or quadrants of your vision board. You can brainstorm below and transfer them to your vision board when you're ready to start assembling it.

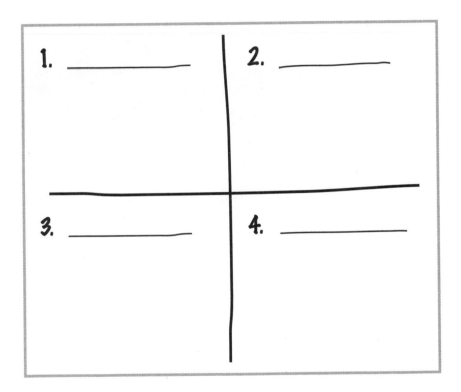

1. _____

2. _____

3. _____

4. _____

As you start thinking about the things you want to manifest into your life, and the items you want to put onto your vision board, think about how they serve your core values and help build your living legacy. Take some time to reflect on how you can realign them if they don't serve the legacy you want to leave.

I once did a legacy exercise where I drew a picture to represent the type of legacy I wanted to leave. I drew a forest with white trees and a light at the end of a long road, meaning that I wanted to be a light to those around me. In the circle on the next page, draw what you want your legacy to look like. Think of this as a visual mission statement. Instead of a group of sentences that are meant to articulate your legacy, draw a picture that feels more like a visual representation of your legacy. You can transfer this image to your board later.

"

Knowing the
difference of what
feels like building
a strong family,
happiness, and
fulfillment is far more
important than doing
the things that might
look like them to
an outsider.

"

03

FEELS LIKE CHRISTMAS

One of the biggest roadblocks I see people encounter when they try to live fully is they get trapped in a lack of awareness of their own life. I see people stop taking stock of where they are in the moment, not paying attention to those places in their lives where they don't have enough of what they need, or noticing the areas where there is too much. Even worse, sometimes when people try to get out of that place, they still don't act with a sense of awareness, and they just focus on the endgame as opposed to laying a path where they need to go.

As we work to live fully, think of it like trying to build a house. When you build a house, you can't just plop the finished house on your plot of land and call it good. You have to first assess the land you want to build on and then lay the foundation for the house. Once that is set, only then can you start constructing the house to get it to that beautiful, finished place. It's the same thing with living fully. You can't skip setting your foundation in your urgency to live fully. And at the same time, you can't rush into living fully if you don't truly know what you want, what you need, and where you are right in this moment.

We all want answers and solutions, but we don't want to stop and truly assess them. And I get it. Sometimes it feels like we've wasted too much time heading in a direction that was wrong for us, so we just want to make things better right away. Or maybe we don't have the courage to really take a hard look at our lives and call out the things that are draining us.

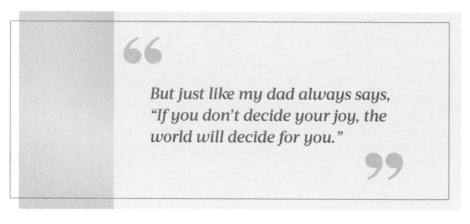

> But just like my dad always says, "If you don't decide your joy, the world will decide for you."

It's up to us to decide what brings us joy and fulfillment, and if we don't take the time to assess our lives as they are right now, what we need to change, and where we want to go, the inertia of a fast-moving world will pick us up and sweep us down a path it thinks is best.

Remember, we're not planning our lives for our social media grid, making sure our lives appear Instagram perfect. The life we want might not look aesthetically pleasing online, and it might not garner photo op after photo op. But when we articulate what we really want in life, we've got to look around and determine if our life right now is getting us where we need to be and if it's honoring the things that are most important to us.

likes 35,000

When we figure out what it is we want by articulating what is important to us—family, faith, health, career, and whatever else—then we can begin actually planning our lives. And we can start making additions and cuts to the things that are in our lives (or not a part of our lives) based on what's important to us instead of simply because we're concerned about how they will look to other people—or we've been doing them for so long they've become familiar.

> **The question you have to ask yourself when you're putting on the outfit, or planning the beach vacation, or going to a trendy hot spot—are you planning the pictures or planning your life?**

It can be so easy to fall into the trap of planning the pictures rather than our lives. During the holidays one year, my friend Erin Loechner encouraged me to refocus how I thought about my family activities. Instead of doing things that *looked* like Christmas, I should plan activities that *felt* like Christmas. So while decorating Christmas cookies might make for a few cute, grid-worthy pictures, the few minutes of fun would be far outweighed by the mess and chaos of two kids wielding sprinkles and icing while hopped up on sugar. To me, that didn't *feel* like Christmas. It felt like stress. **What actually felt like Christmas, however, was piling the family into the car and driving around to look at Christmas lights.** It meant the kids were contained, we were all together, singing Christmas carols, not making big messes, and maybe even indulging in a bit of quiet screen time on the drive home. The outing might not produce a classic holiday photo, but it would definitely create some fun Christmas memories for us all, no mom stress required.

I try to bring that same logic into my everyday life. Knowing the difference between what *feels* like family, happiness, and fulfillment is far more important than *doing* the things that might look like them to an outsider. At the end of the day, you can't live fully if you're living life for someone else, or if you're ignoring the reality of your situation. I know I've already said it, but it's worth repeating: To truly live fully, you've got to take the time to identify what you want and what you need. This means you've also got to see where you're starting from, the pitfalls you might encounter that would slow your progress, and ways you can work to overcome them and build yourself up.

It can take some courage to look at your life, identify what is or isn't working, and articulate the areas where you need more or less—especially if those places take you away from choices that most of your friends or family make. However, the reward will always outweigh the struggle and risks of stepping out of your comfort zone and choosing to live fully. You've just got to be willing to put in the work and take a step of faith.

What are some things in your life that maybe "look like Christmas," but certainly don't feel like it? Brainstorm some ways you can change that.

FOR YOUR VISION BOARD

On the image of the house below, label the parts of the house with the things that will get you to what "feels like Christmas" and living fully. Label the foundation with the things that are bringing you joy, not the things that are stealing it—the things that you need to work to remove from your life. As you build up the house, label parts of the house with things that you either currently have or will work to bring into your life to help build up your life to enter into a place of living fully. You can transfer this image to your vision board when you assemble it.

Reflect

"

It's so easy to look in the mirror and say out loud, "I believe I deserve to live fully," but if your actions don't reflect that belief, it's empty. It stops right there at the mirror, and far short of actual change. So I want you to first know you deserve it, and then act like you deserve it as you're living each day.

"

04

IT'S SHINY. . . . IT'S FINE. . . .

So far, you and I have been looking at pretty big things like our legacy, values, and what we want out of our lives. And sometimes that can feel so big and overwhelming that the temptation to "think small" creeps in and we can't see the forest for the trees, so to speak. So I want to cheer you on here and encourage you to dig a bit deeper, push past those shiny objects out there that can distract you from your goals, and uncover a life that is beautiful and full.

Again, that's why it's important to figure out what it is you really want, not what those around you or society is telling you that you need to be happy, successful, or fulfilled.

Your dreams and desires are important and worthy, even if they might not be the same dreams and desires that your mom, sister, or best friend wants.

And truly living fully means having the confidence to own our destiny and step into the truth of what we want. I want you to experience that confidence too, because your dreams are not only worthy, but when we all live fully and experience the life we were meant to live, they also make the world a much brighter place. So, don't be afraid to speak your mind and own what you want, even if it doesn't look just like someone else's dreams.

The worthiness and beauty in your dreams and desires aren't measured by how many people share them.

I know in my life I've worked really hard to build the family and career that I want. I'm a busy person who loves to be constantly working and experiencing new things. But don't get me wrong, I'm certainly not all business. I love having fun and doing things with my family that have nothing to do with work. But the thing that often surprises people is when they ask me what my hobbies are: I don't really have an answer. Like I said, it's not that I don't have fun, it's not that I don't do things with friends and family, and it's not like I don't travel. But a hobby? I don't have a craft I love to do to unwind, I don't have a favorite sport I leisurely enjoy on the weekends, or some unique-to-me way to pass the time by myself. And it's definitely something I'm paying attention to, but at this point in my life, I can't say that spending an afternoon in a rock-climbing gym hanging off fake rock walls would feel fun to me.

Those kinds of activities don't bring me joy, they don't make me feel fulfilled. All they really do is make me feel like I'm just plain wasting my time. But for other people, like my husband, for instance—his life would be far less full without some of his favorite hobbies. The things that bring him joy, fill his cup, and make him feel truly rested and recharged. But if he was living his life based on what living fully means for me, he'd be missing a huge part of what he needs, and if I was living off what living fully means for him, I'd have a whole bunch of extra that only served to zap my time and energy.

> **You see, if you don't know what makes you happy, then you'll just follow what "they" think should make you happy. We have to do our own deciding. Don't let others point you in a direction of false desires.**

But it can get tricky when we start examining what makes us happy. Because we've got to look deeper than just those activities or parts of our lives that make us smile. Sometimes there are things in our lives that we've tricked ourselves into thinking make us happy, **when in reality what we really like is the attention they get us.** They are what I like to call the "shiny objects." They are the things we use to make ourselves feel more worthy and more important, but really don't serve us at all. If we're finding our worth and importance from anything outside ourselves, it's never going to quite measure up. Identifying those shiny objects can be tough, and getting rid of them can feel even tougher.

Shiny Objects

What are your go-tos when you're introducing yourself to someone? In a five-minute conversation, what do you make sure people know about you? Do you feel the need to drop names and accolades? Do the words come tumbling out of your mouth before you even realize that you've been justifying your existence and worth to a total stranger? Your answers to those questions could reveal your own shiny objects.

If you had to strip it all off and walk around in the world as an average Joe or Jane, how would that feel? Would you want to wrap yourself in your shiny successes as quickly as possible, making sure everyone around you knew exactly what you're capable of? Would you immediately start grasping for the next shiny object you can hold out to show others? It's scary to think about how easily we are drawn to and distracted by shiny objects, but it's also so powerful. These things get a hold on us, and they do it silently, without us noticing. This is your opportunity to notice. And to check in with yourself from time to time to make sure you are not falling into that trap.

What are the shiny objects you're keeping in your life simply because you've led yourself to believe they bring you worth and importance?

> Really start mulling over the ways these things have not only distracted you from achieving what you truly want in this life, but how they've skewed your perspective on your life and your goals.

Fine

On the opposite end of the spectrum is when we **stop** striving for those things we really want in our lives and tell ourselves that we're **fine**. Sure, maybe you feel like something is missing, maybe a piece of your life isn't fitting too well, maybe you feel like you were meant to do something else with your life, but ultimately, you're *fine*. If you read my first book, you know, to me, fine is the new rock bottom because accepting your life as fine means that you've given up in a way. Deciding your life is fine as is and not working to make it truly fulfilling means that you've decided the worth and success of your life based entirely in comparison to other people. You've decided that what you really want isn't the thing that sets your heart on fire and that deep down you feel you've been put on this earth to do. Instead, you succumb to ease and complacency, and have found a life that isn't bad, but it isn't good either. It's fine.

> *Maybe you even convince yourself to feel bad for wanting something other than the life you have now because you look at others in your life, or other people around the world, and you decide that everything is fine just as it is because you see that you aren't struggling in ways your friends might be struggling, or you know you have something someone else would do anything in the world to have.*

Perhaps you've been telling yourself that you're **fine** for so long that you absolutely, wholeheartedly, without a shadow of a doubt believe that it's true and that it is enough for you. Maybe you're thinking, "I can skip the rest of this chapter because my life really is fine. I have no complaints. Life is all right, I guess. Steady. Okay, for the most part. I mean, at least nothing is really wrong." If that's what you're thinking and how you're feeling, I've got a great big red flag in my hand, and I'm waving it for you—hard. Why? Well, the absence of bad is not the qualifier for good.

Fine can come in a variety of flavors, and through the years I got well acquainted with my flavors of fine, and even gave them names: smoky, smothered, complacent, and distracted. Let's take a closer look at each of these and see if maybe you can relate to some of them.

1. **SMOKY:** You know smoky, I'm sure. It's all about smoke and mirrors. We put on a happy face for the world—just keep smiling—but underneath, we are hurting, suffering in a silence that feels unrelenting. Show the best, hide the rest.

2. **SMOTHERED:** This one is just sucking all the life out of you. It's that little voice in your head constantly asking, "Is this all there is?" "Does everybody feel this way?" "Is this how we are all getting through life?" We throw our shoulders back and in our most convincing, confident whisper, tell ourselves we're fine.

3. **COMPLACENT:** This might be the easiest flavor of fine to slide into. We believe that this is just the way our life is, we have no control over it, so why bother even trying to make a change? Relinquishing the controls of our life, we slip silently into autopilot.

4. **DISTRACTED:** This is the most reliable flavor of fine, and the one we can count on every time. We make ourselves so busy that we never bother to check in with ourselves at all, so we literally have no idea how we're really feeling inside. We're all about taking care of anyone and everyone else, except us. Or we're just so busy all the time that we never pause long enough to think about our lives.

As you continue to build a life where you live fully every day, you can't allow yourself to settle for the easy solution. Your desire for the things you want has to overcome the desire to be comfortable, to not rock the boat. Even if it's a difference between 51 percent and 49 percent, **if the thing you want is something that will help you live fully, you've got to want it more than you want to stay comfortable.**

You've got to spot the flavor of fine you've settled into, you've got to spot those shiny objects that have distracted you from the things that actually serve you, and **you've got to start chasing what you actually want in life**.

One big way you can shake yourself out of the place of accepting a "fine" life is to focus on the reasons why you want the things you do. It's one thing to say something like, "I want to get a better job." That might motivate you to update your résumé and search around for new job openings here and there. But if you focus on your reasons for **why** you want a better job–better pay and more flexible hours so you can provide a more comfortable life for your family and spend time with your kids–articulating those reasons will help put a fire under you and keep you focused, even on those nights when you're feeling tired and exhausted from trying to look for a career shift. When we can articulate the why behind our dreams and desires, it suddenly becomes a lot harder to settle for something less than what we know we need in our lives.

So it's time to step away from fine, be bold in saying what we want, and articulate why we want those things in our lives. Once we do, we've set ourselves into motion toward living fully, and we've finally got a direction. So forget fine. Tell me, what do you really want?

What are some of those shiny objects you need to step away from? Write down which flavor of fine you most relate with and how it makes you feel. Now, reflect on how your flavor of fine impacts your joy. If you think you've let yourself fall into living a "fine" life, put it through the best friend test: If your best friend told you they were stuck in "fine" for the reasons you articulated, what would you tell them? Take some time to reflect on why you don't give yourself that much support.

FOR YOUR VISION BOARD

At the end of chapter 01 you started a list of what you desire for your life. Take a moment to read over what you wrote, and explain WHY you desire those things.

Up until now we've been brainstorming, reflecting, and making lists for your vision board; here's where we dig into the how-to of your board. Begin collecting images or ways you can represent your desires on your vision board. There isn't a right or wrong answer, just find a way to represent these things in a way that is meaningful to you. Keep them in a digital file or clip pictures from old magazines and store them in a folder. You can keep adding images as you go. Remember, as I covered in chapter 1, we want to put those ideas on our board in their fully realized state, so get as specific as you possibly can.

Reflect

_____

_____

_____

_____

_____

_____

_____

_____

_____

_____

_____

_____

_____

_____

_____

_____

"

Just remember.
You've got two choices.
You can either say,
'Good morning, Lord!'
or 'Good Lord, it's
morning!'

"

05

TOO MANY COOKS

I have two amazing children, and as I'm writing this I'm pregnant with a third. But between my second child and the one I'm currently pregnant with, I had four miscarriages. They were so out of the blue and devastating, but the first two didn't derail me completely from believing that I could successfully carry another child. I tried to look at the glass half full; I'd been able to carry two successful pregnancies to term before, so I still had hope. However, after my third miscarriage, I started to get worried. As part of the typical recurrent loss protocol, I began seeing more doctors to figure out what was going on. I went to so many specialists to figure out what was causing me to lose all these pregnancies back-to-back, and each of them identified a different cause and recommended I embark on a different treatment plan to get my body ready to carry a pregnancy to term. My mind was buzzing with the opinions of all these doctors, my own feelings of fear, grief, and sadness, and my increasing frustration in trying to figure out what was the right next thing for me to do.

And in the middle of it all, I miscarried again. This time I was even further along. I was much closer to my second trimester than I had been with my other three losses, and I started to realize that if I was going to try to get pregnant again, I needed to sort some things out in my head. I knew that I wanted to have another baby, and I knew my desire for another child was stronger than my desire to **stop** trying out of fear, even if it meant risking another miscarriage. But I knew I couldn't keep going on like this, seeking too many answers.

I realized if I was really going to have a shot at the family and the life I knew I wanted, I was going to have to get clear on the path I wanted to take. I couldn't keep up this pace of listening to the input of so many doctors. Not to discredit the medical community at all, but in my desire to find a solution I was drowning in the advice, conflicting ideas, and treatment plans from at least five different specialists. I needed to quiet the noise, and I needed to make a decision I could stick with and at least try.

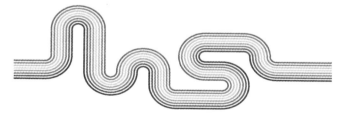

The input of too many people, however trustworthy, wise, and reliable they may be, can overload us and make us fall into a place of indecisiveness, paralyzing us and keeping us from making any definitive moves in our lives. There were too many cooks in the kitchen, and I needed to get a bunch of them out if I was ever going to figure out what I should do next.

I needed to shift my perspective, and big-time. I realized I needed to choose a path forward, a medical team that felt right, and a protocol that made sense and that I could follow. I needed to quiet that overwhelming feeling of fear that I'd never be able to carry a pregnancy to term again, or that I would make the wrong decision and the wrong moves. I needed to stop trying to find the "correct" solution and find a doctor and a plan that worked best for me and my family. Because partially following a bunch of different plans and never really giving one plan my all was making me feel increasingly overwhelmed.

So, I decided I would listen to the guidance of one of my doctors, and I'd follow their protocol. I'll be honest, **I wasn't sure if I was making the right decision, but I was confident that it was time to make a decision.** With things quieter and a path mapped out ahead of me, I finally was able to make some real progress toward my health goals and expanding my family—and I was finally able to carry a healthy pregnancy.

Obviously, not everyone reading this is dealing with the input of tons of doctors as you try to carry a healthy pregnancy to term after a string of miscarriages. I could easily identify who the extra cooks in my proverbial kitchen were. But you might not have that scenario. You might be dealing with advice, criticism, or even encouragement from family, friends, the internet, mentors, and teachers. You might be trying to sort out helpful input from general societal or cultural pressures. You might be unsure of the best path forward, so you're desperately reaching out for as many sources of advice as you can to find the absolute perfect, correct path. If the noise and indecisiveness are coming from all around you rather than a handful of people, how can you work to quiet the racket so you can make some definitive decisions toward living fully? Just like I did when I was going through my year of loss and health diagnoses, it's all about dialing down the noise and making a confident choice.

However, with so much noise around us all the time, it's not only hard to pick a path, but it can also be hard to even make out which way you need to go because you're feeling so overwhelmed that you can't even begin to focus on solutions, or anything other than negativity. There are lots of ways to cut through the noise. Sometimes it's being decisive like I was or sometimes it can be shifting your perspective.

Wallowing in negativity and indecisiveness have no place in living fully.

Shifting perspective can be a major tool to help you. Life might feel a bit wild or out of control, but I'm happy to let you know that you are totally in control of your perspective, and shifting it starts the moment you wake up. It's like my grandma once said, *"Just remember. You've got two choices. You can either say, 'Good morning, Lord!' or 'Good Lord, it's morning!'"*

If we allow ourselves to be swayed by the opinions of others, let ourselves get swept away in a frenetic pace or a tidal wave of depressing news, or let that noise and negativity stop us from making decisions, we can't possibly live fully. We've got to shift our perspective, focus on the positive, make a conscious choice to live every day fully, and to start the day saying, "Good morning, Lord!"

But it's not as easy as simply greeting the Lord in the morning or spouting off popular sayings like "Good vibes only." Because, for whatever reason, sometimes it's easier to live with a "Good Lord, it's morning" perspective. Negative stories are often easier to tell others—misery loves company. But our negativity can not only impact our day, it can impact others.

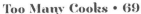

"

For the times when I do get stuck in negative thoughts or disappointment when reality doesn't match my expectations, I do what I think of as an emergency prayer. It's like a grounding prayer where I ask God to help me turn this around because I want to do the best work I possibly can, and I don't want this to stand in my way. It goes something like 'Please enter into this situation. I need you here in my life now. I cannot do this on my own.' Then I have faith in the process and know that every negative or hard thing leads somewhere positive in my life. That allows me to release the low-energy thinking and shift my entire perspective.

"

Like with anything in life, shifting our perspective is hard work, and sometimes it doesn't feel like the natural way to respond to a situation. But the moment we start doing it, our lives will massively shift and change for the better. We've already talked a lot about owning the fact that you can achieve your dreams, and that you're worthy of the good things you want. And that's so true, but that doesn't just mean telling yourself that you're worthy. It also means that when things start going sideways, when life gets hard, or when something unexpected changes up your plans, you remember that even in the middle of the chaos, you are still worthy of living fully, and you still have what you need to achieve those dreams you have for your life. You deserve to live fully when things are going well **and** when things get a bit complicated.

Take a second to think of the first ten things you do in the morning. How many of those things are life-giving, and how many of those things let in unnecessary noise, skew your perspective for the day, or even steal your joy? It is up to us to quiet the noise around us and realign our perspective so we can move forward and make decisions toward living fully.

But if our perspective is fueled every morning by listening to all the negative things happening in the world, if our brains are buzzing with input from tons of different sources regarding decisions we have to make, or if we're just doom-scrolling so much we start out our day feeling hopeless, we can't live fully. We can't clearly identify what we need and want out of life, and we can't get to a place where we feel confident enough to make a decision, stick to it, and continue moving forward in the best direction for our life. But once you realize you can control your perspective and you can control the direction of parts of your life, a lot can change.

Look at your life and your circumstances right now. Is your inner monologue set to a negative autopilot and it's flying you right into the ground? When something doesn't meet your expectations, do you immediately start losing altitude? You've got to acknowledge that you're flying the plane, and the minute you start pulling back on those controls, you can pull yourself out of that rapid descent.

Jot down a few ways to redirect yourself if you find yourself falling into a spiral of negativity or hopelessness.

I create that internal shift.

When I was deciding what to do after my fourth miscarriage, I realized that I didn't need to have the right answers. I just had to find what I felt was best for me, and I had to make a decision and commit to it. Like I mentioned, when I was deciding which doctor to stick with, I wasn't confident I was making the right choice. I knew it was entirely possible that I'd end up circling back, making a new plan, and trying again. But what I realized was in overloading myself with information and increasing the noise so I could illuminate the perfect path forward, I was just making my life chaotic and completely stalling my momentum. The thing I was in control of was my perspective and my internal life, and if I wanted to move forward in my journey to have another baby, I'd have to take some definitive steps. So I made a choice. I didn't know if it was the "right" choice (or if there even was a right or wrong choice), but I knew I had to do something. I encourage you: Once you've made your choice, if you realize you're not on the right path once you've seen it through, make another choice and fully commit to that one.

When you want to manifest good things, reality will get in the way sometimes. There's disappointment in these tough moments, but there's double disappointment when you focus on the negative and overlook good aspects too.

Focusing on the noisiness of life and letting that shift our perspective away from our goal of living fully is one of the quickest ways to stop us from living the life we want. And it's so much more than choosing to be cheerful. Another cliché thing you've heard, I'm sure, but it works, is to focus on our blessings rather than the negative parts of our lives. When we shift our perspective to the ways we've been blessed, as opposed to focusing on the hardships, we can see the opportunities around us, and we can find a way out of tough situations.

Do you feel overwhelmed with too many cooks in the kitchen? How does their input make you feel, and how does it keep you from making decisions about your life? Think of ways you can reduce the noise, and some ways you can feel more confident about making decisions in your life.

When you're in more of a "Good Lord, it's morning" state of mind, how does that perspective impact your ability to articulate what you want and need, and make decisions? How have you gotten out of that place in the past?

FOR YOUR VISION BOARD

Go back and look at the dreams and desires you've written and collected for your vision board. We worked on identifying how they align with our core values, but take another look. Is there anything that maybe adds to the noise of your life? Take a moment to reflect and remove the things as you need to.

Reflect

_____ _____
_____ _____
_____ _____
_____ _____
_____ _____
_____ _____
_____ _____
_____ _____
_____ _____
_____ _____
_____ _____
_____ _____
_____ _____
_____ _____
_____ _____

mindfulness

So Happy
Together

heal

Serve

In the first chapter I told you we'd get
into the how-to of your board. Now it's
time to dig in. You've done the work of
setting goals, reflecting on your legacy,
and collecting images. Now's the time
to move things to your board.

1 First, choose your format. If you're going old-school, you can use a large poster board. Or if you're doing a digital board, create a new page and use the cut and paste feature.

2 Second, revisit the core values you listed in chapter 2 and decide on sections for your board. Group your images to go with each one.

3 Third, put the images of those things you've collected or drawn on your board.

4 Finally, you don't have to glue anything down yet; your board is not complete. But start to piece it together now. Keep adding photos and art as time goes on, and slowly see your vision of a fuller life come alive!

"

I create the right tone for the day by reminding myself that I choose my pace. In other words, I don't always have to be in such a huge hurry.

"

06

GLASS AND RUBBER

We've all heard that we need to pay attention to what we're bringing into our lives, but often we ignore the speed at which we're doing that. Because even if we've managed to quiet the number of voices and opinions crowding our brain, if we're constantly moving too fast, things can still feel out of hand. It can be hard, even with the best of intentions, to keep a positive perspective when everything feels like it's moving a thousand miles a minute. Life gets busy, and it can seem like the only way to get everything done in a day is to kick off your morning by running yourself ragged. The thing is, even on a busy day, we can't give our best when we're running on fumes and the pace isn't sustainable. I'm not going to say that your life won't get busy, but it's always important to remember that you are the one who sets the pace for your day, and you are the one who gets to decide what that pace will be.

I create the right tone for the day by reminding myself that I choose my pace. In other words, I don't always have to be in such a huge hurry.

It can feel tempting to wake up and immediately start checking e-mails, leap out of bed to get ready for work, start cleaning your house, or making breakfast for your family, but I encourage you to start your day at a pace you know is sustainable. If you've got your day packed with so many things that on a regular basis (because we all have days that get crazy) you HAVE to run yourself ragged to get everything done, it might be time to start looking at what you've got on your plate and what might be worth stepping away from.

In my book **Living Fully,** I wrote about an analogy that my friend Jessica Turner brought to my attention. It originally came from former Coca-Cola CEO Brian Dyson. He said that, in your life, you're juggling glass balls, which are the most important things, and rubber balls, which aren't as important. If you drop the rubber balls, they'll do what you might expect a rubber ball to do—bounce back. But if you drop the glass balls, they won't bounce. They'll crack, or even shatter. The idea is to strive for balance and to focus your attention on the important things, so you don't drop the glass balls. The glass balls are the parts of your life that you value most deeply. The rubber balls are the things that don't matter as much in the grand scheme of life.

While everyone's version of living fully will look a little different, there are a few "glass ball" tasks that we can all agree on—things like keeping your family safe and cared for and maintaining your health.

GLASS BALLS	RUBBER BALLS
☐ Family	☐ Household Chores
☐ Health	☐
☐	☐
☐	☐
☐	☐
☐	☐

But think about everything you're juggling in your life. Without giving it too much effort, I'm sure you're able to come up with one or two things that you probably treat like a glass ball when it's really a rubber ball, right? Maybe it's people or projects that you're putting your time and energy into that no longer serve you. Maybe it's chasing a dream that was never something you wanted to begin with, but a trusted individual in your life told you it was something you should pursue. Maybe it's something that started as a glass ball, but the level you're maintaining it in your life is unsustainable. For example: Instead of keeping your house clean you're trying to keep it at Pinterest-level perfect without dust, clutter, or stains, ever. Or maybe it's something a bit more fluid like creating a life that, going back to the analogy from chapter 3, *looks* like Christmas rather than *feels* like it–forcing family photos, planning family adventures that you know your family won't enjoy but you feel pressured to experience, or planning dates with your spouse that will look good in pictures and in stories but aren't fun in real life.

I think this message about balance is one of the simplest lessons I've been taught, but it's as complex to navigate as the stars in the sky. The concept is easy. It's the practice that's hard. That's why I need so many reminders about it.

Finding that balance, knowing what is a glass ball and what is a rubber ball, is vital to living fully. My dad is one of the wisest men I know, and if there is one thing I can always count on him to talk about when it comes to living fully, it's finding balance in your life. He constantly reminds me of this when he imparts his wisdom in the form of chicken-scratch notes he's written to me over the years.

"Balance is one of the most important things in life," he'll write. Then he'll include a list of words like "work," "family," "faith," "passions." Then he'll go on to say, "At times, you will get out of balance, and this will bring on hardships. When you lose your balance, you lose yourself. So, you have to find that balance again."

A huge component of living fully and articulating what it is you really want is deciding which of the things you're juggling are the rubber balls, and which are the glass ones. And the best way you can ultimately decide where to put the tasks in your life, and what things to label glass balls and what things to label rubber balls, is to look inward. Chances are, you've got some of your glass and rubber balls mislabeled. I know there are times in my life when I certainly did, and it's something I constantly have to take time to reflect on.

It's also important to remember that when we mislabel the balls in our life, we can focus on protecting the wrong things, and we let the important stuff suffer. My friend Jessica and I had a long conversation about how the problem starts when we mistake the glass balls for rubber balls. Our families? If we keep flitting around our homes obsessively cleaning up instead of sitting down with our people, that's a glass ball dropped. Our marriages? If we stop communicating with our spouse and asking what we need from each other because we're scrolling social media or too tied up in work, that's a glass ball dropped. Our careers? If we spend all our time working to have a job that impresses others but doesn't work to build a lasting, fulfilling career that empowers us, it's yet another glass ball dropped.

Taking the time to really examine how we prioritize things in our lives and to constantly check back in to make sure our glass balls and rubber balls are still properly labeled is one of the major ways we can start and continue to live fully. In our lives, those glass and rubber ball labels are going to shift and change depending on our season of life.

Remember living fully means living the life **you** were designed to live. I can't tell you what you need to add to or subtract from your life. You've got to trust yourself and your gut, and follow your heart when it comes to looking at the glass and rubber balls you're juggling.

Deciding what tasks are glass or rubber balls means examining everything on our plate, articulating what we want and what we need, and filtering out (or simply not prioritizing) those things that don't serve us or don't guide us toward our goals.

> If we don't take the time to figure out what parts of our life are precious and what things in our life can be knocked down on the priority list or dropped entirely, we won't be able to truly live fully because we'll be juggling and protecting things in our life that don't matter and don't serve us. It can feel like a lot of work, and can be overwhelming, but it is worth the work. You are worth the work, I promise you!

*Reflect on the pace you choose for each day.
Does it affect your mood and the perspective you
have for the entire day? What makes you feel
like you have to keep moving so quickly?
Does your daily pace feel empowering,
or is it stopping you from living fully?*

FOR YOUR VISION BOARD

Are there any things in your daily routine that you need to add or subtract to help you achieve the things you put on your board?

Take another look at your vision board in progress and see if there are some things you maybe need to remove from the board, or create more blank space on your board to foster a daily rhythm of living that is more sustainable. (Dr. Tara Swart suggested I make mine 1.5 times bigger to create space, so that's an option too.)

Reflect

"

Because when a curveball comes our way, we are caught off guard. We often think it is the absolute bottom, the lowest, the worst, most life-altering moment in life. We think it's all over and we'll never be the same. How do we stand on our own two feet when our life feels altered in such a deep way? Well, we just do. Eventually. Because with time, the pain always passes. It's always one step forward and then another. Until we're walking on our own again.

"

07

PIVOT!

I'd love to tell you that once you start realigning your perspective, cutting out the noise, defining your core values, manifesting, and allowing yourself to live fully that nothing will ever get in your way. But that's just not the reality of the world we live in. The unfortunate truth is, even if we're doing everything right, when we're in the right mind-set, living as fully as possible, life can throw us a curveball. And sometimes, those curveballs can feel so devastating that they can completely unravel us and derail any hopes, vision, or plans we had for our future.

Because when a curveball comes our way, we are caught off guard. We often think it is the absolute bottom, the lowest, the worst, most life-altering moment in life. We think it's all over and we'll never be the same. How do we stand on our own two feet when our life feels altered in such a deep way? Well, we just do.

Eventually. Because with time, the pain always passes. It's always one step forward and then another. Until we're walking on our own again.

We have bumps in the road, curveballs, or **downright wrecking balls** that can be utterly devastating in our life. The curveballs come along much more often. I pray to God that the wrecking balls are few. I'm not here to tell you every tragedy or injustice you faced or will face is something that you'll come to be grateful for later. But I can say that every single curveball, wrecking ball, or form of rejection has always guided me where I need to go. And I know that will be true for you. Sometimes we eventually discover that, in truth, they were exactly what we needed, and we may even feel grateful for them. We look back and think, "Thank God it didn't work out." But not always. A job loss. A serious illness. A death. Those are things that can not only feel devastating, but they can also truly feel like the end. But it's in those moments that we must remember: **This isn't the end,** and in the same way our pain can be the catalyst for strengthening our character, our darkest moments can lead to our life's purpose.

First I want to tell you about someone who endured a wrecking ball and then we'll take a look at curveballs later in the chapter. If you know my story, you know I've walked through disappointment, rejection, and addiction, but hands down, the person I always point to when I think about making it through the trenches, seeing light at the end of the tunnel, and finding their way out of darkness is my sister, Jade. If you've read my book or listened to my podcast, you've heard her story. But I want to spend some time in this book diving a bit deeper into what she went through, **because I've discovered that we are all searching for that comforting feeling of knowing someone else has been steeped in the darkness, and found their way back to light, and back to themselves.** If you're in the thick of it right now, and you're thinking, "I'd love to live fully, Mallory, but right now I'm just trying to survive," this chapter is for you, my friend.

My sister felt in her bones that she was meant to become a mother. She had so much trouble getting pregnant and was considering starting in vitro fertilization to conceive. If you know anyone who's gone through IVF, you know what a long journey it can be, and Jade wasn't sure if that was the path God had for her. My sister is such a strong woman of faith, so she prayed for a sign to give her some direction about what to do next. When a friend told her she had a vision of God holding her, my sister took it as a sign to stop exploring IVF and trust that He would make her a mom. And not long after, she got pregnant. Everything was fine until around twenty weeks when she discovered her baby had a heart defect. It was a serious condition, but the baby's ultimate prognosis was a good one. As time went on, however, things got more and more dire. After the baby was born, he spent thirty-four days enduring surgery after surgery—on a roller coaster from hope to despair—and ultimately just over a month after Jade's son, Blaise, was born, he passed away.

None of it made any sense. Why had God told Jade He was holding her if her baby was ultimately going to be taken from her a few weeks after birth? And why was it happening *now*? Jade was going through this in the early days of COVID, so not only was she going through a massive tragedy, but she was also going through it largely alone because the hospital didn't allow her and her husband (and especially not the rest of her family) in the hospital room at the same time. So even though we were all there for her as much as we could be, we weren't able to physically be there, and that was devastating for all of us on top of everything.

Hopefully, you aren't walking through something as tragic as the loss of a child. But regardless of what you're dealing with right now, how you move through the moments of frustration, darkness, and pain, how you deal with it is going to dictate what you do on the other side. And I know it's hard, especially when the pain or loss is truly soul-deep, to try to pick ourselves up and move forward.

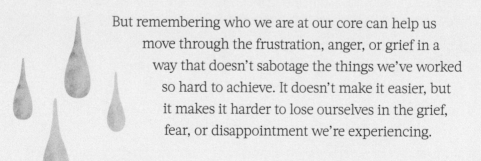

But remembering who we are at our core can help us move through the frustration, anger, or grief in a way that doesn't sabotage the things we've worked so hard to achieve. It doesn't make it easier, but it makes it harder to lose ourselves in the grief, fear, or disappointment we're experiencing.

"

Because when we walk around wearing a cloak of rejection, loss, or disappointment, we make our next move from that place, rather than as who we are at our core, our original, **and** we set ourselves up for more problems.

"

While they aren't the same as wrecking balls, curveballs can knock us off balance and leave us on shaky ground. When a curveball comes before we do anything, in those moments we have to remember that though our lives have changed, we are still the same person. Look back at those core values and that legacy you want to live. Those things are still valuable and worthy, even when your world feels as though it's been turned upside down. I want to encourage you to remember who you are and cling to that.

We must remember to trust the process, and trust that we aren't meant to stay in those valleys forever. It's part of why we identify our core values and make them a part of our vision board. We need to not only be reminded, especially in those hard times, of what we're working toward, but also why we are doing so.

For my sister, she was still a woman of faith who believed deep in her soul that she was meant to become a mother. And losing Blaise didn't change that. But it would have been so easy for her to experience that gut-wrenching pain of losing a child and say from that place of loss, "Clearly, I'm not meant to be a mother. I never want to go through this again," and stop all attempts at having a baby.

My sister easily could have lost herself, and she could have let the pain overtake her. She could've done whatever she could to try to numb the sting of loss and constant ache in her heart every time she thought about the precious baby she knew for such a short period of time. She could have seen that grief coming, and done everything to fight it, numb it, and ignore it, refusing to do the hard work of acknowledging the loss and striving to heal the pain. But she didn't, and because she chose to feel the pain, heal, and then move forward, her life changed in ways I don't think she could have ever imagined.

I love how Glennon Doyle puts it: "Whatever we use to numb the pain hurts us more than the pain would have. Let it be. It'll pass and leave you bigger, better, kinder, softer."* I believe that's true. Numbing, covering up, or ignoring pain just creates a new set of problems, and it doesn't ever allow for the pain to pass naturally. Instead, it hangs around in the background, lurking, lingering, and threatening us. When you deal with it head-on, the pain will begin to lessen.

---

* Glennon Doyle (@GlennonDoyle), Twitter, April 15, 2015, 9:40 P.M., https://twitter.com/GlennonDoyle/status/632728496595410944.

I'm not going to say that a loss or a curveball isn't still going to hurt. Unmet expectations and loss still hurt, and it's okay to grieve and take some time to heal. **What is key is to not stay in that hard place.** Feel your pain, process it, and then begin healing and slowly pulling yourself back up.

> 66
>
> *The way to get your feet back on the ground in these circumstances is to first reconnect with your values so you can then make decisions as your more authentic self. It requires a certain amount of discipline to set aside the emotions of the situation long enough to say, "Here's what is important to me. Here are the things I value above all else. Now, coming from those values, what is the next step that feels right and true to who I am?"*
>
> 99

For my sister, getting back on her feet meant pivoting from sessions with a grief counselor the hospital recommended to starting work with a life coach who was ready to help her work through her grief. Now I'll be the first one to say that I love therapy, and I'll sing its praises till I'm blue in the face. But my sister knew that what she needed in that time wasn't someone to talk through her pain, but to help her map a way out of it. So she and her life coach talked about her feelings, what she wanted, and they structured a daily schedule to keep her moving and climbing out of the pit she was in. More than that, once she was able to heal enough, she was even able to grow from that pain and tragedy.

I've not been through a wrecking ball like the one Jade has been through, but I've had my fair share of curveballs, and I have now gotten to a point in my own life where I can honestly say that when some form of adversity comes my way, even in the middle of that adversity, I can say, "Thank you for what this is teaching me, and for where I'm being guided." Granted, there are times when I say it through gritted teeth, or in a tone that is not super thankful. But I do mean it because I know that it is through these things that I have found the gift of a full life. And with a powerful example like my sister to follow . . . how could I not work to see the light at the end of the tunnel when my sister was able to find her way out of what I think is one of the most profound losses a person can experience?

It doesn't stop the pain, and it doesn't fix everything, but feeling grateful for what we're learning can help keep us grounded when life doesn't go as we planned. It can also help keep us focused on the truths we hold about ourselves like our values, faith, and our desires. It can keep us secure when the winds pick up around us and it can help us see a way out, even when the path forward is hard to follow.

A lot of us have a really narrow window of tolerance for adversity, especially if you were blessed to grow up in a pretty positive environment like my sister and me. So when we visualize our lives and how we're going to achieve the things we want most, we don't really think or even take time to consider the hardships we'll encounter. Unfortunately, we all know from experience that we'll face hardships even if we're doing everything right. But when there is a path forward that honors the full life we want to lead, it can help us be a bit more prepared to deal with curveballs when they come.

We want the good stuff, but we're not expecting the hard stuff, and sometimes we're not even willing to deal with the hard stuff. But if we understand the fact that hardships are a part of life, and that we will experience hard things, it can help us reframe our perspective, attitude, and the way we deal with the dark times. It might feel like we're lowering our expectations, but when we accept the fact that curveballs, pain, and unexpected complications are going to come, we can be more ready for them, and not let those hard times totally derail our lives.

The other amazing thing about the hard moments, however challenging they may be, is that life on the other side can be even brighter. My sister now has a beautiful son, George, and she's happier and healthier than ever before. She views each day as a mira-

> "Any time we get knocked off our normal, stagnant, baseline existence, it's an opportunity to reclaim our lives. This is your one life. Do not leave it unlived; instead, aim to hit it out of the park, curveballs and all."

cle, she's stronger in her faith than ever before, she has more confidence in who she is meant to be, and she just lives more intentionally than she did before. Also, I feel her marriage is even stronger for having weathered such a storm together with her husband. Of course, she still misses Blaise—we all do. But working so hard to find the light in the middle of the darkest season made her life even richer now. She appreciates life so much more, and it was all because in her darkest times, she got up, put one foot in front of the other, and kept walking.

When you find yourself in that place, facing a curveball, or even just a crossroads, remember who you are. **Remember what makes you *you* and what gives you that spark, that firework. And remember that your circumstances don't change you.** Then do your best to make decisions from that knowledge, and put one foot in front of the other. It might take time, and it won't be easy, but you will find your way out of that darkness, and your life could shine brighter than it even did before.

Sometimes a curveball means we get the opportunity to reevaluate our lives, or adjust some ideas or desires that are no longer serving us. Remind yourself of a time a curveball hit your life by writing it down. Then, think back on what lesson you learned from it once you made it to the other side. These reminders are great to refer back to when you face a curveball again.

FOR YOUR VISION BOARD

In whatever way is most meaningful to you, write out some truths about who you are, and a few ways you can remind yourself of this in the middle of a crisis. If you're having trouble doing this on your own, you could find a trusted friend or family member and ask them to help you identify three or four things that are true about you. How could you represent those words on your board?

Brainstorm a few things that are helpful to you when you're working through a dark period. Is it having someone to talk to? Is it creating a schedule to keep yourself moving through each day? Is it your faith? Is it getting away for a bit to refresh your perspective? Brainstorm a few ways you can give yourself the help you need when you're struggling to put one foot in front of the other in the midst of a hard time. If it's a person, add their picture to your board, or if it's a setting, add an image of it to the board.

Reflect

"

I want you to take what you've discovered within these pages and finally grab ahold of the kind of life you want to live. I'm living proof of a life that could have gone one way or stayed exactly where it was. But it didn't. Because I chose a bigger life. I wrote this book hoping you will too.

"

08

STAY AWAKE

Now what? Well now is the good part. The part where we put these things into action. You're on the launchpad and the countdown is about to begin. The drive behind my original *Living Fully* book and brand has always been to guide people to bigger lives, and I know from my own experience that it's the small things that get us there. The shift in changing your perspective, the pause in assessing your life, really deciding what you want and need without the inclusion of those shiny objects, how to quiet the noise, being decisive, and dealing with curveballs. Now I hope this has been a bit of a wake-up call for you to truly take control of your life and actually begin to live fully. But I don't just want to wake you up, I want you to stay awake.

"

*I want you to
take what you've
discovered within
these pages and
finally grab ahold of
the kind of life you
want to live. I'm
living proof of a life
that could have gone
one way or stayed
exactly where it was.
But it didn't. Because
I chose a bigger life.
I wrote this book
hoping you will too.*

"

It's time to take things out of the hypothetical, it's time to stop thinking about making change, and it's time to start taking actual steps to make change happen.

This is where the rubber hits the road and where we can finally start shifting the direction of our one and only life. So much of what actually gets us to this location are the actions we take once we have the clarity, and then continuing to choose the actions and tools over and over again as our life tends to slip back to baseline.

Now that you've created your vision board–if you haven't glued or taped it all down go ahead and do that or, if you're working on a digital board, print out a copy. Now, take a moment to look at what you've created and really visualize your life looking like it will when the things you've put on your board come true. Really take the time to see every detail you can about the life you're envisioning for yourself, and allow yourself the time to feel gratitude for what is to come.

Really allow that gratitude and confidence to flow through you and allow yourself some time to experience what it will feel like when the things you have put on your board are there waiting for you. Now in the space on the next page write a quick reflection on how that made you feel.

One of the reasons I've gone on and on about the day-to-day nature of living fully is because it can be easy to lose sight of our goals in the middle of the mundane and the ordinary. I don't want you to just make a vision board, tape it to the wall in your closet out of sight, and then just continue living the same way. It's so important to create reminders for ourselves to check in on a regular basis and assess our life. We're done with a "fine" life, and we're here to live fully every day, and that means keeping our eyes on what we want in our lives.

So, once you have your vision board created and you feel ready to start living fully every day, I want you to think of a place in your home that you can put your board. Find a place that isn't easily overlooked so you can keep your vision for living fully in the forefront of your mind. You're going to have those days that feel exhausting and you're going to have those days where you feel like the entire world is against you and you'd just rather slip back into "unaware and checked out." But when you check out you miss out. And I don't want you to miss out on a pretty amazing life. I can't let you do that.

> **Feel free to add and subtract, or completely rearrange the visuals on your vision board whenever you want. This is a gift and a tool we can use to remind us of where we're going when we're lost in the dark. And it's a tool that can help aid in neuroplasticity, your brain's ability to change.**

If you're done letting the world dictate your direction, and you're done just living life, barely making it by, then it's time to get started. It's time to go **all in** on yourself. It's time to go **all in** on life.

That's why this is your stay-awake call rather than your wake-up call. We're creating a totally new lifestyle together. We're going to put markers in place to check in on our new lifestyle and ensure we're still heading where we need to go.

So right now, I want you to take a moment and set a few alarms in your phone or reminders on your calendar. One for three months from now, one for six, one for nine, and one for a year. Choose times when you can take a moment to reflect and think about where you're at. I want you to answer these five questions right now, and then answer them again in the next three, six, nine, and twelve months.

When your alarm goes off, or your calendar reminder pops up, I want you to go stand in front of your vision board, ask yourself these questions, and consider if what you see in front of you still reflects the life you want for yourself.

1 Does my life align with my core values?

2 What are the glass balls in my life, what are the rubber balls, and what are the things I'm juggling that have been mislabeled?

3 Am I living every day striving to live in legacy mode, and also am I achieving those things I've visualized for myself?

4 If not, what changes do I need to make?

5 Are there areas in my life where I need more or less of something?

As you journey through this year and you are able to finally grasp those things on your vision board, be sure to take the time to **celebrate** how far you've come. Remember, living fully isn't just about reaching a destination, but I want you to be proud and celebrate when you reach one of those big goals you set for yourself. It's a reminder that this stuff actually works! Achieving goals is always a big deal, and I don't know about you, but I always love a reason to celebrate. Obviously, celebrating with your family or community is wonderful, but adding a date or a little symbol next to the item on your vision board when you've reached it can help your board not only be a reminder of where you're going, but what you've achieved. So on those days that feel hard, slow, or you feel a little lost, you can remember that you've come further than you may feel in that moment. Because once you decide you're all in and you start living fully every day, you are going to be amazed at the life that will eventually unfold!

Look again at your vision board. It's a gift to yourself that you can be proud of. You're manifesting a meaningful life now and in the future. Living fully is the gift that keeps on giving if we keep on giving it to ourselves. Never stop. Until the very last beat of your heart, keep giving yourself that gift. This moment represents your chance to take what you've discovered in these pages and finally grab ahold of the kind of life you want to live. Now, let's go all in.

About the Author

MALLORY ERVIN, author of the national bestseller *Living Fully*, is a Kentucky-grown, Nashville-living dreamer who had a roundabout way of arriving at today. From her time in the Miss America pageant to being a three-time contestant on *The Amazing Race*, Mallory turned her passion for sharing her love of fashion, beauty, and life into a platform for impact. Today she runs a global lifestyle brand she founded in 2016, hosts the *Living Fully* podcast, where she encourages and inspires her dedicated followers to seek joy and live fully, and appears across platforms ranging from Instagram to YouTube, sharing her life and message of living fully. She and her husband, Kyle, have three children, Ford, Shepherd, and their new baby, Sunday.

About the Type

First designed for Chilean newspaper *La Tercera* in 2010 by Portuguese typeface designer Dino dos Santos, the Acta family is a clean and fresh type system, while conservative enough for newspaper setting.